This book belongs to:

_____

Published by Lennox® Publishing
PO Box 28266 Chattanooga, TN 37424, U.S.A.

in conjunction with

No portion of this book may be reproduced, stored in a retrieval system,
or transmitted in any form or by any means — electronic, mechanical, photocopy, recording,
scanning or other, except for brief quotations in critical reviews or articles —
without the prior written permission of the publisher.

This title may be purchased in bulk for educational, business,
fund-raising, or sales' promotional use.

For information, please e-mail
requests@comeandreason.com

Cover design, graphics and layout: Louis Johnson
Editing: Mirra Huber

2020
Printed in U.S.A.

ISBN: 978-0-9858502-9-6

Title: God Is Love
Author: Stephanie Land

God Is Love!

I can see!

I am the light of the world!

WRITTEN BY **Stephanie Land**
& ILLUSTRATED BY **Louis Johnson**

God IS Love.

God, Jesus, and the Holy Spirit live together as One in Love.
Love is patient and kind, always gives, and thinks of others first.
God shows us His Love in all that He does.

Every time He creates, it is always with love.

This is God's design for life - the
circle of giving. In fact, love is the basis for life.

One neat way to see this is when we breathe.

Did you know that the air we breathe out gets soaked up by plants?

The plants then turn it into clean air that we breathe in. We GIVE what the plants need, and then the plants GIVE us back what we need! This happens over and over, all day and night, never stopping.

It shows us how the circle of giving keeps us alive, and it is a great example of how God's design-law for life works.

The Circle Of Giving

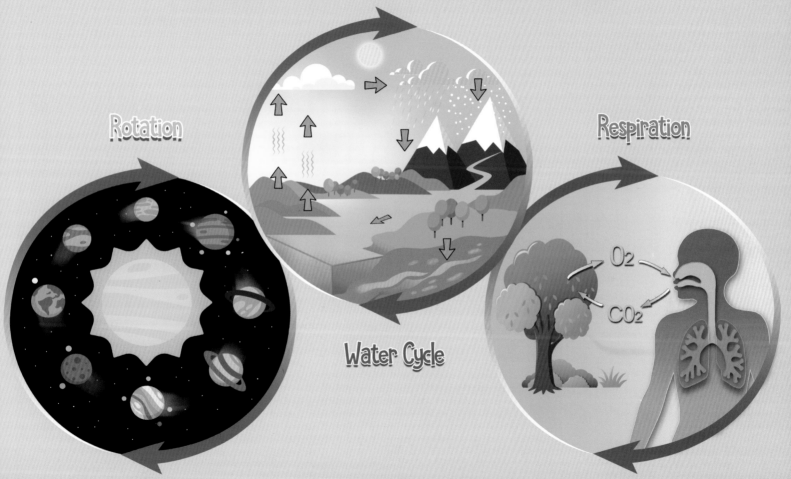

Rotation

Water Cycle

Respiration

Long ago, before Earth was created, God and angels lived together in Heaven. Their entire existence was based on giving and receiving love.

But one day, the greatest angel, Lucifer, chose to become selfish and didn't want to love anymore. Instead of thinking of others, he only thought of himself, which is the complete opposite of love.

Lucifer started telling lies to the other angels. He said that God wasn't fair and therefore they couldn't trust Him.

The angels were confused and wondered if what Lucifer was saying was actually true!

Lucifer's lies caused a war in Heaven! This war wasn't a battle of strength and power, and it didn't use weapons, like knives or guns.

Instead, this war was raging in the heart and mind of every angel.

It was a war of ideas about WHO God really was.

Lucifer became known as Satan, which means Deceiver. His lies caused the angels to question if God could be trusted. So, God showed them the truth of how He does things.

He revealed His design for life in a really awesome way!

With the angels intently watching, God used His amazing power to create the Earth in just six days. He did this to show how the Law of Love works to keep life going. Most of the angels were thrilled and praised God for it

But Lucifer was not at all happy and told more lies about God, saying,

PUNISH YOU

"Of course God is powerful, but if you don't obey Him, He will punish you for it!"

However, God was ready to provide even more evidence: on the seventh and last day of creation week, God revealed His character and method of love - He simply rested!

This wasn't because He was tired, but because He gives real freedom.

God paused to give all His intelligent children plenty of time to think and then to decide for themselves who was actually right. God revealed that even though He possesses so much power, He never uses it to force anyone to believe or obey Him. He always gives us freedom. Imagine God saying, "Look at what I have created. See how My love works. Take some time to think and decide whom you believe: Lucifer or Myself."

Earth was created to be the crowning jewel in God's universe, where His character of love would shine most brightly.

God designed Adam and Eve flawless, with freedom to make their own choices, even if those choices would lead them to not trusting Him. God wanted them to become mature and perfect by always choosing love and rejecting selfishness. This would show the angels how God's Kingdom of Love operates.

In the beautiful Garden of Eden that God had created for Adam and Eve to live in, they enjoyed His company every day. They knew God truly loved them and only wanted the best for them.

But one day, Satan appeared in the garden as a brilliant, dazzling serpent with shiny, golden wings. He hissed into Eve's ear that God cannot be trusted. Sadly, she believed Satan's lies and shared them with Adam, who also chose to distrust God.

Immediately, they became afraid and tried to hide from God. From that very point on, Adam and Eve were filled with fear and selfishness, otherwise known as sin-sickness.

They didn't have love or trust in their hearts anymore.

Yet if you remember, life cannot exist forever without love.

Adam and Eve's sin-sickness set them on a path towards death.
Because of their choice to distrust God, all humans are born with this sin-sickness - even you and me.

God was incredibly heartbroken that His creation had become sin-sick, but He also knew that He could save them. God had a plan to heal their sin-sickness.

God's plan was for Jesus to come to Earth as a human-baby.

He could be tempted and feel pain like we do, yet Jesus would live a perfect life, always choosing love instead of selfishness.

By doing this, He would not only show people what God was really like, but He would also become the special medicine to heal our sin-sickness.

Satan didn't want people to be healed from their sin-sickness. He didn't want them to know God's love. He hated God and did everything he could to separate people from God.

Sadly, by the time of Noah, almost the whole world chose to follow Satan. Everyone was selfish, violent, and turned against God - everyone except Noah. So, when the flood came, the only people who trusted God and got on the ark to be saved were Noah and his family.

Come on people, a flood is coming!
It does not matter who you are.
Get into the Ark while there's still time!

Hundreds of years passed, and people still didn't understand that their sin-sickness could be healed if they just turned their hearts to God and His love.

To help them see their true selves, God, through His friend Moses, gave the people a mirror for their hearts. We call it the Ten Commandments. The people could look into this mirror and see their sin-sick symptoms very clearly.

When we have a sickness like the flu, our symptoms of fever, cough and runny nose help us figure out what's wrong. Then we can go to the doctor for medicine that can heal us. As we take the medicine, the sickness goes away, which automatically makes the fever, cough and runny nose go away too!

Likewise, the Commandments show us the symptoms of our sin-sickness. Our symptoms may include disrespect of our parents, disobedience, lying, cheating, stealing, or jealousy of our friends.

God, our Heavenly Doctor, gives us Jesus – the cure for our sin-sickness, which will also take away our sinful symptoms!

Unfortunately, God's people used the Ten Commandments as a set of rules to follow, instead of using it as a guide to point out their sin-sickness and lead them back to Jesus to restore love in their hearts.

When Jesus came to Earth, many people followed the rules and acted like they loved God, but they didn't really know God, and didn't have love in their hearts.

The Scriptures told about a coming Messiah who would save the people, but they thought this Messiah's mission was to fight off their enemies.

When Jesus – the true Messiah – came as a humble man, changing hearts of sinners and healing the sick, the religious people rejected Him. In fact, they wanted to kill Him! They accused Jesus of breaking God's law, even though it was the religious people themselves who didn't understand or follow God's Law of Love.

It was at the cross that this heavenly war over ideas about God came head-to-head: love against sin-sickness, God against Satan.

Who would win this war? Would Jesus give in to the crowd's teasing and act to save Himself? Or would He give His life to provide the cure for the world's sin-sickness? Would He use power to destroy His enemies? Or would He choose love and freedom, and prove that Satan had lied about how God uses His power?

Jesus selflessly gave His life in perfect love. He was glad to be our medicine, because He wanted us to be well and understand that God can be completely trusted. Jesus showed us that God always acts in love: He gives us true freedom, even to the point of letting the beings He created kill Him.

At the cross, the angels in Heaven, who had the opportunity to be with

God every day, saw for themselves how trustworthy God really is.

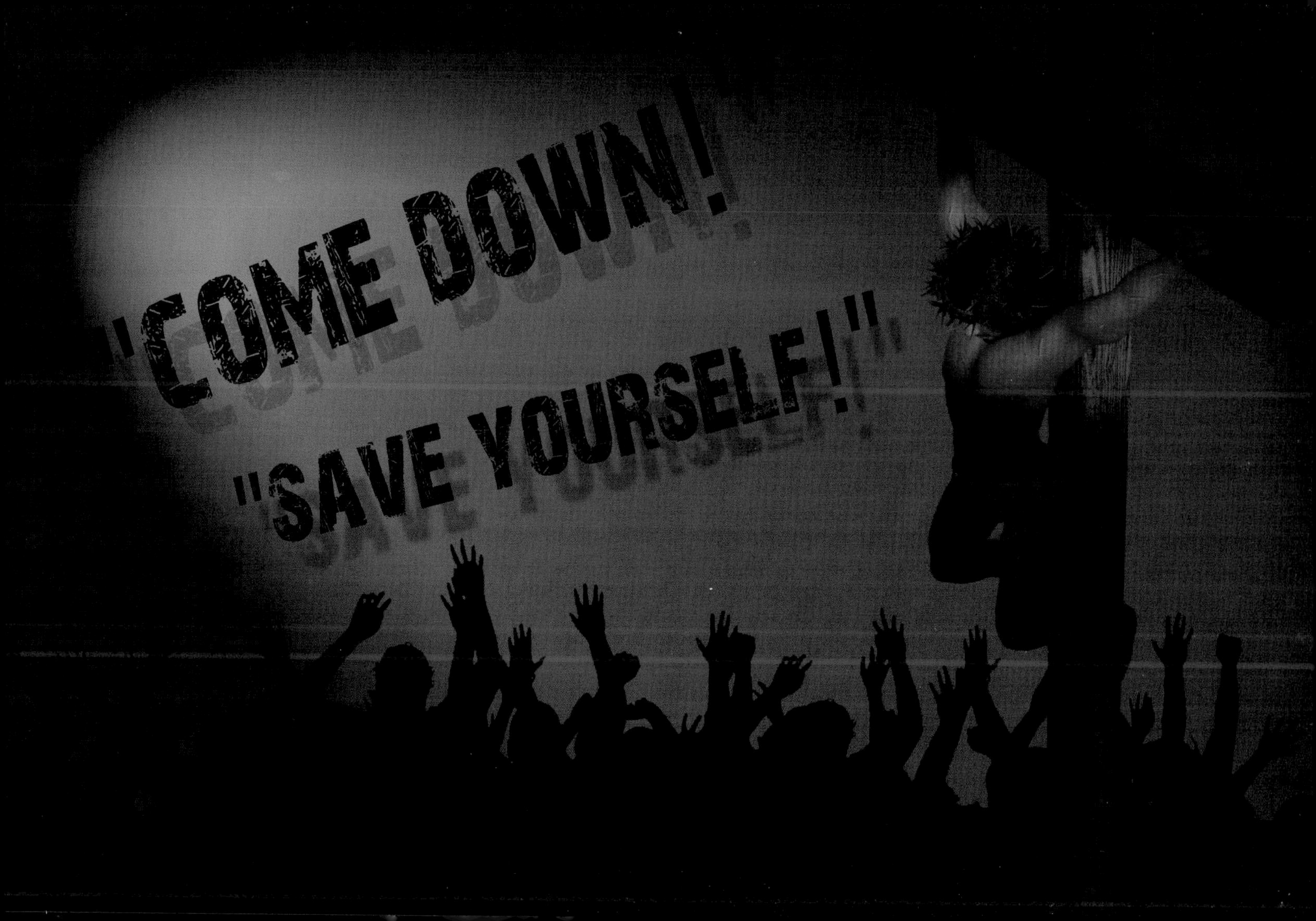
"COME DOWN!"
"SAVE YOURSELF!"

Because of Jesus' selfless act of giving His life in love, we can become like Him! All we have to do is to realize we are sin-sick and invite Jesus into our hearts to heal us. The Holy Spirit's healing powers of Truth and Love can help us change our wants and desires. Our sin-sickness can be healed, and we can have love in our hearts. This is just the way God designed us all to live!

If we were once mean to others, with Jesus in our hearts we can choose to be kind. If we used to tell lies, now we can choose to be truthful. If others make us angry, we learn to forgive.

God is good, and everything good comes from Him.

Some people think that God will have to kill those who don't follow His rules, but that is Satan's lie! God's Law of Love is God's design for life. It is not a made-up set of rules that must be kept under threat of punishment.

When you have love in your heart, you want to give to help others find happiness, and you never want to hurt them. This is the way God designed life to work. But when you have sin-sickness in your heart, you only want to protect yourself, even when it hurts others. Sin-sickness hurts us too; and it is not God but sin that is the cause of eternal death.

As you get older, you will realize that brushing your teeth keeps them healthy, while not brushing them will lead to cavities, pain and disease.

This is the natural design-law of tooth hygiene.

Natural design-laws have natural consequences when disobeyed.

Wow! Brushing my teeth sure makes them look and feel great!

Likewise, our sin-sickness goes against God's design-law for life.

Selfishness is the opposite of love.

Thankfully, God is healing and restoring us back to His original, perfect design.

He can enter our selfish hearts and make them beautiful and selfless.

This is God's justice, or doing what is right.

But we need to choose to trust Him, and be healed and restored to God's perfection.

Maybe you're thinking,

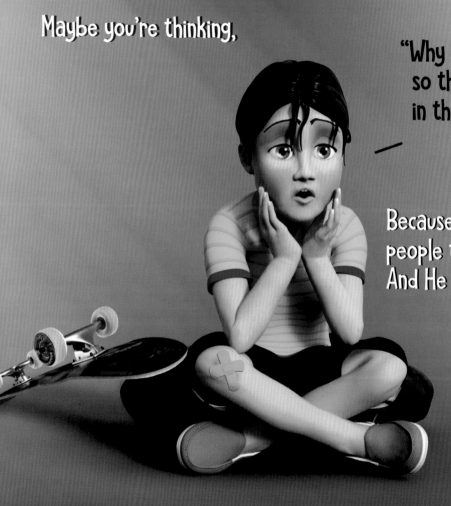

"Why doesn't God just heal EVERYONE, so there would be no more sin-sickness in the world?"

Because God will never use His power to force people to be healed against their free will. And He won't threaten us to love Him, either.

Love cannot exist without freedom to choose.

Would you want to play with that friend under the threat of harm?

Or would you question if they were really a good friend?

In the same way, God can't win us to love and trust by threatening us or forcing us to choose His ways.

One day soon, Jesus will come back to take us to Heaven. Heaven is a place of truth, love and freedom.

But some people wouldn't like to live there, because their hearts never learned to love truth, and they rejected healing.

God wants all of us to be healed from our sin-sickness, but He won't force people to choose something they don't want - even when the natural result of unhealed sin-sickness is eternal death.

The only pathway to life is through the healing that our God of love freely offers to us.

Will you open your heart to love truth, trust God, and let Him heal your sin-sickness?

Let's talk with God

Dear Jesus, we want to be like You, full of Your love and life. Please come into our hearts and heal our sin-sickness!

We want to be ready for Your return, so help us to grow in truth, make good choices, and to choose love always .
Amen.

"Whoever does not love others more than self has not been healed and doesn't even know God, because God is love."

1 John 4:8 – The Remedy NT

For more information on God's character of love and design laws, visit:

www.comeandreason.com

comeandreason
MINISTRIES

Stephanie Land is a stay-at-home mom to her two children, Lennox & Dexter.

With her husband, Michael, they strive to help their children grow in love and trust of their Creator God.

When Stephanie is not busy managing their home, she enjoys bookkeeping work and volunteers at her children's school.

She is a first-time author, who wrote this book because it was put on her heart.

Stephanie is passionate about sharing the message of the God of Love that has changed her life.

Louis Johnson (aka Uncle Louie), is a US-born illustrator, designer, teacher, sculptor and puppeteer with over 18 years of experience in working with youth and young people.

He studied Graphic Design in California and commenced his career at Loma Linda University Medical Center.

Louis then moved into software design both in the USA and Australia which spanned 35 years. After retiring from software design, he hosted a Christian radio program called, "The Larger View - A Program about God's Character of Love as seen in Jesus Christ".

Uncle Louie is owner and founder of "ReLoveolution!", a program which uses uniquely created puppets, props and engaging tasks, to help people learn more about God's "Circular principle of receiving and giving".

Louis lives in Queensland, Australia with his wife Sonja, their son Liam and much-loved dog, Ruby.